IMAGES OF ENGLAND

ELLAND
REVISITED

IMAGES OF ENGLAND

ELLAND
REVISITED

BRIAN HARGREAVES

TEMPUS

To Michael, Olivia, Ethan, James, Adam and William for all their support during the preparation of this book.

First published 2006

Tempus Publishing Limited
The Mill, Brimscombe Port,
Stroud, Gloucestershire, GL5 2QG
www.tempus-publishing.com

British Library Cataloguing in Publication Data.
A catalogue record for this book is available from the British Library.

ISBN 0 7524 4145 0

Typesetting and origination by Tempus Publishing Limited.
Printed in Great Britain.

Contents

Acknowledgements

My thanks go to Dr Bruce Bain for his information on Stainland and to Margaret Drinkwater for her interest in the Greetland section.

David and Emily helped with preparing the text and I thank Adam Watts, for his help with editing. Margaret helped with patience and proof reading.

My thanks also go out to the people too numerous to mention, who have shown an interest in this compilation.

Introduction

'History is bunk'. Henry Ford was certainly entitled to his opinion but many people in the area covered by the Greater Elland Historical Society would disagree with his view. Their interest, research and hard work over many years are testimony to the fascination with history and, in this instance, predominantly local history. We need to grasp the importance of the past and learn that history forms an essential part of our culture. It should be cherished and deserves to be enjoyed.

The Greater Elland Historical Society was formed in 1974 by a group of local people and it could just as easily have been named The Stainland or Holywell Green Historical Society. The first president was Dr Roderick Bain of Stainland and the inaugural chairman was Albert Moody, who was sub-postmaster at Holywell Green.

Once the society was established the members felt that some sort of emblem was appropriate and suggestions were considered. This emblem now adorns the letterhead of the society:

To understand this emblem we must go back to AD 43 when the Roman invasion of Britain began. The 9th Legion, the one that concerns our area, was stationed at Pannonia, on the Danube in Hungary. They marched 400 miles to the Rhein to join the 2nd, 14th and 20th Legions and then assembled at Boulogne under Aulus Plautius to prepare for the forthcoming invasion.

The legion was built up of ten cohorts, each of 480 men. There were therefore four legions of 4,800, making a total of 19,200 soldiers available for the assault. Attached to the 9th Legion was a tribe called Breuci. These were not mercenaries but auxiliaries conscripted from the conquered territories and absorbed into the legion.

The invasion was successful and resulted in the capture of Colchester, after which the four legions separated and moved into different areas. The 9th Legion advanced to York about AD 80 and they were responsible for the construction and maintenance of the roads between York and Manchester, together with the forts along the way. One of the forts was Slack at Outlane and for its construction a kiln was built at Grimscar to produce roof tiles and pottery.

The auxiliary attached to the 9th Legion must have been responsible for this work in approximately AD 120 because they stamped their name on the back of the tiles in much the same way that today's brick manufacturers stamp their bricks. Tiles have been found on the site at Slack with the mark COH IIII BRE that indicates the 4th Cohort Breuci.

After the Romans left Britain the forts were abandoned and forgotten but in 1590 men digging for coal discovered the kiln at Grimscar. In 1954 the site was excavated by boys from Fartown School following the discovery of some tile fragments in the wood. In 1964 the Tolson Museum of Huddersfield and Heath Grammar School carried out further excavations. All this in some way explains the symbols on the society's emblem.

There are numerous connections with Roman Britain within the area covered by the society, and one of the more notable is the discovery of a unique Roman altar at Thick Hollins in Greetland in about 1597.

As a society we are often faced with enquiries, from all parts of the world, about forebears, property and people. We have people who specialise in military matters, Elland families and St Mary's church. We try to cover most aspects of the history of our local area.

If Henry Ford were here, I would ask: 'Is history bunk?'

Brian Lawrence Hargreaves
2006

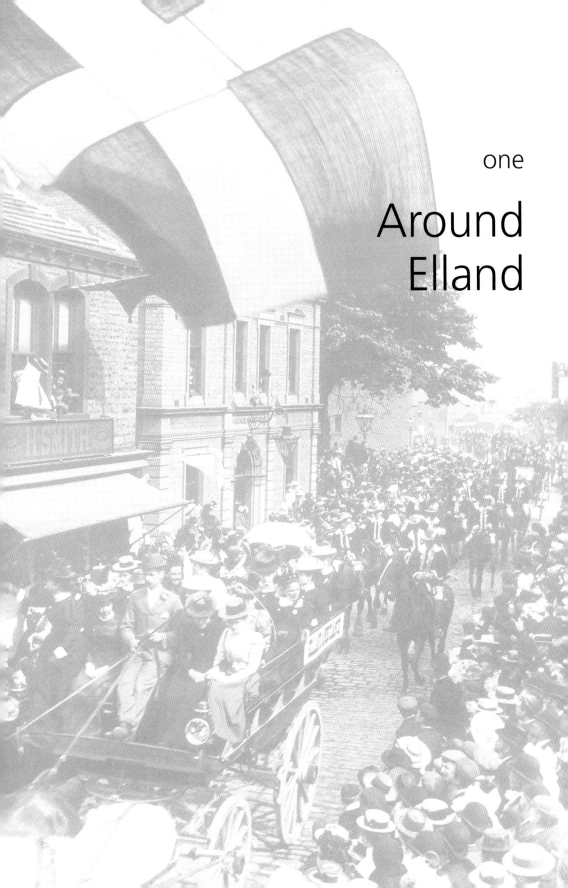

one

Around Elland

Elland Wharf in 1893 was a hive of activity. Barges are loaded and unloaded, many having journeyed from Hull. The footbridge in the centre allowed towing horses to change from one bank to the other. The Station Hotel is on the central left with Dewhurst's Valley Mills behind.

Smithies Albert Mills in Saddleworth Road, or Bank Bottom, are situated centrally in this panoramic view at Lower Elland. The roads, river and canal line up obligingly. The Calder and Hebble Canal, the River Calder, Saddleworth Road and Long Wall can be seen (left to right). Taken in the early twentieth century, the photograph still shows property at the junction of Long Wall, Hullen Edge Road and Westgate. The property halfway down Long Wall is still occupied.

A constable stands alone while others line up for the photographer in Southgate, *c.* 1898. The street is unusually devoid of traffic.

The building to the left was demolished in 1935 and was Boxhall. When the hall was being knocked down the sundial was removed and placed at the National School, but this was lost in the upheaval after the fire in 1942.

The cottage in the centre of the picture was at one time a public house called the Crown and Anchor. This, somewhat uniquely, gave us three licensed premises together; the Malt Shovel was to the left and the Royal Hotel to the right. Quite a number of public houses were situated in this area and they included the Staff of Life, the Jolly Boatman and the British Workman. The magnificent Brittania Buildings replaced the cottage.

Mighty sycamore trees dominate the junction of Park Road and Exley Lane, with the entrance to the railway goods yard on the right. Lilleys Dyeworks and Halifax Road are on the left.

Very nearly the same viewpoint but looking in the opposite direction, i.e. towards Brighouse, road-widening operations are in progress with the railway goods yard entrance behind. The avenue of agreeable looking gas lamps leads us to the railway bridge over Park Road. The Station Hotel waiting to greet weary travellers is on the right.

The latest technology is brought into play during the strengthening and widening of Elland Bridge in 1896/97. Donkey engines, piledrivers and pumps are all in use in this shot. The newly strengthened and widened bridge was reopened on 13 November 1897. Since the earliest mention of the bridge in 1199 it has been repaired and replaced a number of times. Notably in September 1615 it was swept away by a flood and rebuilt in 1617 at a cost of £484 15s 4d.

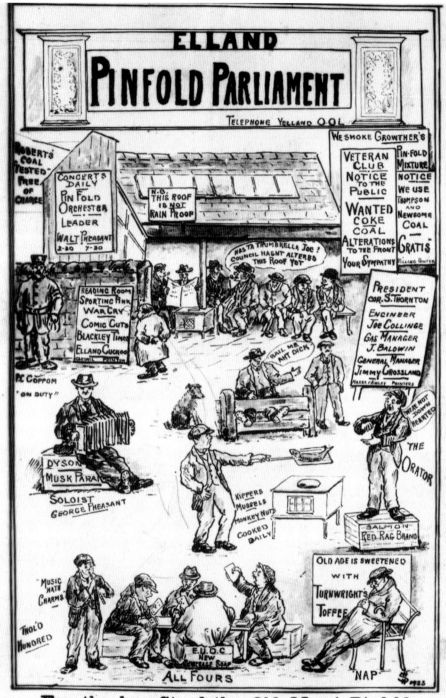

For the benefit of the Old Mens' Pinfold Annual Outing.

This card extols the attitudes and grumbles of the Elland Pinfold Parliament, which was housed in the Towns Rooms – formerly Elland Gaol – at South End. ('Robert's coal tested free of charge').

Workers at Wilkinson's Brickyard, Blackley, 1934. Front row left are the Midgley boys, who lived at Ainley Bottom. Second row, fifth from the left is Arthur Chadwick, sixth from the left is Mr Noble, who was manager, and seventh from the left is Edward Pepper who became manager. Third row from the front and second from the right is William Taylor.

Elland Town Hall Square before work began on Elland Victoria Swimming Baths. Although more than one hundred years have elapsed, the surrounding buildings are virtually the same.

Elland Road leaving Brighouse was subject to a calamitous incident of subsidence. Tag Lock is behind the trees to the left.

Dick Taylor's cart. George Ray is sitting at the back on the far side. The man at the front with the white collar is Randolph Horsfall and the boy behind George Ray's elbow is Arthur Morton, who later lived at Elland Hall.

People stand four or five deep to watch an Elland carnival procession of the early years of the twentieth century. The ambulance in the foreground has just reached the junction of Victoria Road and Southgate. A mounted contingent follows and coaches of firemen in turn follow them. At the left, H. Smith (now an optician) tells us he is a 'Hosier, Glover, Shirt and Stay Maker'. The Council Offices are to the right of Smith's shop.

Victoria Avenue and the houses and gardens are in pristine condition in this snap of 1910. These properties were the first council houses in Elland.

The Central Picture House in Coronation Street is still operating as the Rex Cinema, one of very few independent cinemas in the country. Central Hall is on the right and Box Hall Road has not yet been made to the left.

Victoria Road in 1966/67 and the Talbot Garage awaits demolition. The entrances to New Street and Brooksbank Street are boarded off and the building behind was Talbot House. This name survives with the block of flats situated off Victoria Road.

Kagan's Gannex Mill, Sam Lumb's Perseverance Mills and the Perseverance Works of James Lumb can all be observed in this aerial shot of Dewsbury Road. Thomas Street, Quebec Street, Westbury Street and Heathfield Street are also visible.

Awaiting passengers in Dewsbury Road, this omnibus has one of many destinations displayed. This road was the original route to Wakefield and subsequently London.

People standing at the junction of Elizabeth Street, Roseberry Street and Burley Street watch as a carnival procession of the 1920s passes. One of the wooden buildings housed a shoemaker's business and Charles Dyson, later to have a shop in Victoria Road, was apprenticed there.

The condition of Upper Edge, Dewsbury Road, is atrocious as horse-drawn vehicles try to negotiate the muddy surface. For heavy goods wagons, as many as ten horses were needed to reach The Black Bull (The Pinfold) before returning to Elland.

An example in South Lane of how four two-storey cottages can be adapted to serve as a textile mill. Two extra floors have heightened the left-hand dwellings. Access is achieved by way of an outside stairway and two blocked 'tekkin in' doors can be plainly seen. On the left is the entrance to Elland Finishing Company and Illingworth's Mill is to the right.

The chairman of Elland Urban District Council, Cllr W. H. Eastwood JP, opened the baths on the 22 November 1902. They were built at the astronomical cost of £6,000. Visible in the distance are the towers of Elland Wesley Methodist church.

Park Road is the main artery to Brighouse. The surface of the road in this 1903 postcard is well rutted. The Calder and Hebble Canal is to the right and the mill of cotton spinner Benjamin Whiteley is to the left of the road. The chimney of W.T. Knowles, pipe makers, can be seen in the background.

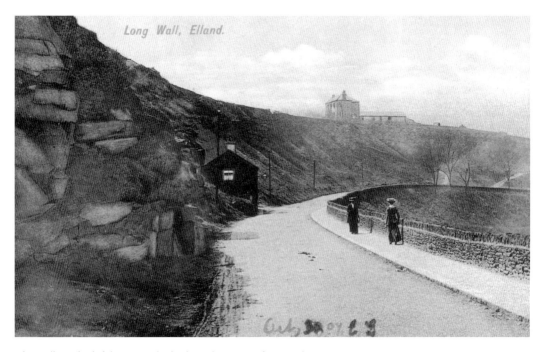

The wall on the left has yet to be built in this view of 1907. The card is addressed to 'Mrs Albert Townsend, Hollyn's House, Greetland', and was posted in Outlane. A family named Bailey occupied the house pictured centrally for a period.

With many of the men away during the First World War, the women of Elland, like many other towns, took up the challenge of taking on occupations that had previously been male dominated. Here we see post women, bus or tram conductors, farm workers and munitions workers among many others.

Harvest time and the corn sheaves stand in orderly fashion. Saddleworth Road (Bank Bottom) runs centrally towards Greetland. The covered runway of the rope works can be seen on the left. The person giving directions has it slightly wrong if they think the X situates Halifax.

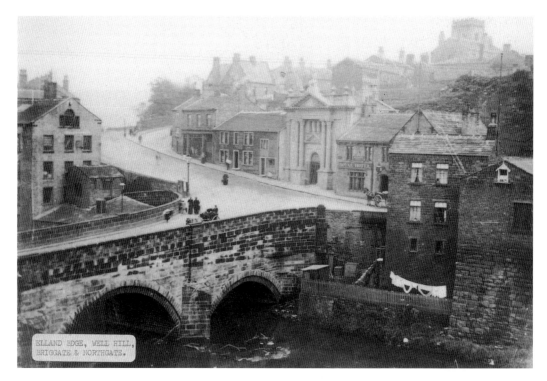

A wide-open view of Briggate and part of Elland Bridge. Millgate leaves the bridge and passes through the Kiln End Mills complex towards Calder Cottage. The horse waits patiently outside the Royal Hotel and the dye house on the right has a number of samples out to dry.

The Wesleyan's first chapel at the corner of Eastgate and Castlegate was opened on October 4 1808. Its twin doors faced into Eastgate. As it was close to Dog Lane it became known as Dog Loin chapel. A new chapel, the building still standing, was opened on 4 October 1892. The last service was held there on 7 July 1974.

Around 1910 and this gang of workers lay an electric cable in Savile Road. In 1900 an order for compulsory electric lighting was given by royal assent and the areas to be lit were: Southgate from the Town Hall to The Cross; and from The Cross up Westgate to the Fleece Inn. The centre of Elland was lit up on 17 October 1903.

The 'old' Rising Sun stands at a right angle in Jepson Lane prior to 1914. The ancient Fleece Inn can be recognised by its gable ends over the high wall. The Rising Sun was demolished and built further back to allow the road to be modified for the tramway, which was extended from Elland to West vale in 1914.

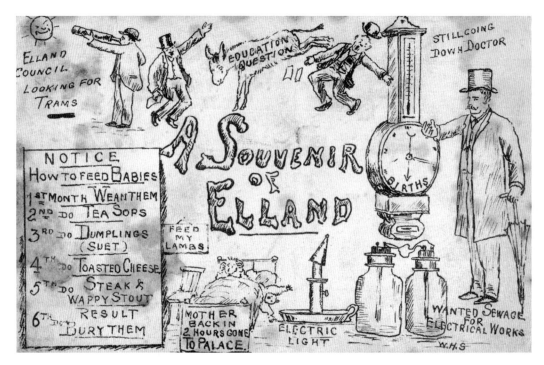

Dated 1905, this card has Elland looking for trams wanting sewage for the Electrical Works. We see how to feed babies, and 'mother will be back from the Palace in two hours'.

Brooksbank Street in 1961 before it was swept away by compulsory purchase. The gable end is of The Brooksbank Institute, which was Elland's grammar school in a previous existence. The sign above the car prohibits cycling on the footpath, which is an ancient footway from Stainland to Elland. The child is Michael Hargreaves.

Kew Hill at Blackley is now totally changed with the encroachment of the M62 motorway. To the left is Kew Hill chapel. The row of houses included the Friendly Inn. The building on the skyline centrally is Ainley Hall.

Substantial buildings at the junction of Church Street and Huddersfield Road. Bishop's Grocery Store is central and one of the basements was occupied for a time by the 'Knight of the Needle', Albert Hanson. The tall buildings on the left housed the White Lion.

The junction of Westgate, Hullen Edge Road and Long Wall before the alterations of 1914. The chap on the ladder might be awaiting the arrival of the Keystone Cops.

Opposite and above: These three snaps try to capture the pandemonium suffered by neighbours during a fire at George Lumb's cotton-spinning mill in Quebec Street in 1912. A number of residents had to evacuate their properties.

The cottages with the hoarding were demolished and a new building was erected that abutted with Cooper kitchen's Moorgate Chambers. The pharmacy now occupies this space. A. Dyson of London House advertises his mourning clothes; Elland also had a Manchester House and Liverpool Stores.

Everyday life continues but these residents of Newcombe Street still find time to pose for the cameraman, *c.* 1904.

two

Canal and River

Three young men lounge beside the river in this aspect looking towards Elland. The chimneys of Lambert Dye works and the Albert Mills of Joseph Smithies can be seen. The postcard was printed in Saxony from a photograph by Henry Spencer of Southgate, Elland, *c.* 1904.

The lock and railway bridge with Woodside Flour Mill and chimney in the background.

Some Elland people will remember the half-sunken barge, which was at Elland Bridge. The Station Hotel and the Gasworks dominate the background, 22 June 1957.

The Carey family of Elland operated a number of barges on the Calder and Hebble and the Aire and Calder canals. Here Douglas Carey (front left) supervises the launching of *Gwendoline* at Ledgard Bridge in 1953.

Barges line up at the Woodside Flour Mill in 1898. The canal traffic was in direct competition with the railway system and with road transport entering the age of the internal combustion engine, movement of cargo by barge began to wane.

By the 1960s barges were transporting pleasure seekers. Here two vessels negotiate the Park Road locks. The mill of cotton spinner Benjamin Whiteley can be seen in the background.

three

Royalty

One of the oldest surviving photographic images of Elland is this of 1863. Taken at The Cross, the decorated pillar surrounds a gas lamp standard and gas jets are mounted on protruding arms. This feature was erected to celebrate the engagement of Edward, Prince of Wales and Princess Alexandra of Denmark. An illuminated display was placed on the front of the nearby Savile Arms and it said 'God Bless The Prince of Wales'.

This timber arch was built on Elland Bridge to welcome King George V and Queen Mary during their Coronation Tour of 1912. The man sixth from the left is Mr John Edmund Worth, who was responsible for the electrical work on the arch.

On Sunday 15 November 1931 – Armistice Sunday – the Earl of Harewood, the King's son-in-law, visited Elland to dedicate a new standard to the Elland and Greetland branch of the Royal British Legion.

The Earl of Harewood lunched at Woodlands on Park Road with Lt-Col. W. F. Denning and his family. Pictured are (left to right): Lt Col Denning; Brigadier General R. E. Sugden; The Earl of Harewood. Centrally are the Sugden daughters. Mrs Sugden is front left and Mrs Denning is on the right. At lunch the earl famously asked for a second helping of Yorkshire pudding.

Opposite above: As part of his coronation tour, King George VI passed through Elland on Wednesday 20 October 1937 on his way to Halifax. The crowd were positioned at the north end of Elland Bridge.

Opposite below: Princess Elizabeth and the Duke of Edinburgh are photographed in Huddersfield Road, Elland on 29 July 1949. The royal car is just passing the Salvation Army yard.

Right: His Majesty King George VI and Queen Elizabeth are pictured at Shibden Hall with the mayor, Cllr C. Hodgson JP.

Below: The Earl of Harewood formally opened the extensions at Brooksbank School on 27 November 1970. The earl unveils the plaque watched by the countess, with headmaster George Locke on the left. Second from the right is Jack Howarth, rector of Elland.

The Prince of Wales visited the Lowfields site in Elland on 4 December 1987. It was hoped that his visit would encourage efforts to utilise the area for business and industrial use. The power station ceased generation in 1991 and was demolished shortly afterwards. This area is now the Lowfields Industrial Estate.

Prince Charles chats to people and scholars of Old Earth School on the approach to Elland Power Station.

four

Greetland

A view of Greetland from the Bull Fields. Sunnybank Hall is visible centre right, with Sunnybank Drive climbing the hill towards St Thomas's church on the horizon.

Looking over West Vale towards Greetland. St John's church, West Vale School and North Dean Mill are on the centre right and the streets of Lindwell are situated centrally.

A view of Lindwell from The Mount. The entrance to Lindwell on Road End is at the extreme right. Facing this area is the Star Inn and centrally there was another public house, the Shoulder of Mutton. Lindwell Methodist chapel is in the background.

A continuation of the previous photograph, taken about 1901. Coronation Street is to the right but John Street has yet to be built. The house with its door set at an angle is No. 1 Road End. In the background are the stone quarries where stone for many local properties had been obtained.

Looking up Rochdale Road. The entrance to Lindwell is on the right. This road is, in part, a Roman road and it was one of the main routes from Elland into Lancashire and Rochdale.

Some boys and girls enjoy playing on the gateposts of the old tollhouse in Martin Green Lane.

Greetland and West Vale from Woodside, taken from a postcard posted in Halifax and timed at '3.45pm SP 30 07'. Brow Bridge at West Vale is on the extreme right, with Victoria Mills pictured before its water tower was built. Lindwell and Hoults Lane can be seen in the middle distance.

The mighty Brig Royd Mill is seen in this aspect pictured from behind 'Jack's' fish shop at Brow Bridge.

Looking at the café and fish and chip shop from Rochdale Road. The Victoria Mills, now with water tower, are behind. This mill is now occupied by Andy Thornton of Architectural Antiques.

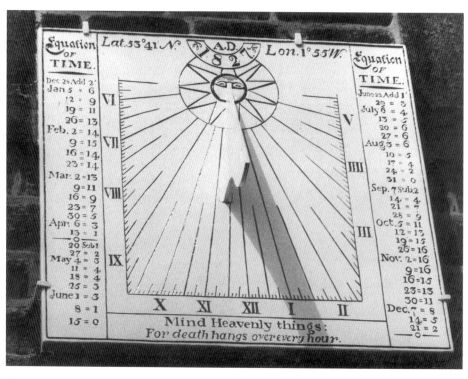

This sundial was situated at Greetland Wesleyan church at Cross Hills. We are reminded to 'Mind Heavenly Things: For Death Hangs Over Every Hour'.

The North Dean and Prospect Mills are prominent here. The extension to North Dean was built in 1919 and this card is postmarked 14 January 1918. Stainland road leading to Calder and Hebble can plainly be seen behind the North Dean Mill water tower.

This much later card shows the North Dean extension is completed. Lumby's Boiler Making Plant lies beside the River Calder and Lambert Dye works are creating steam. Long Wall and Saddleworth Road are in the foreground with the 'Ha'penny Bar' disappearing towards Halifax.

A Huddersfield tram reaches the terminus at West Vale in Saddleworth Road. This route was extended from Birchencliffe and then Elland in 1914.

Claye House – Claye with an 'e' – is a typical 'Halifax house' with gable ends and a through passage. Although giving the impression of a complete build it was erected in stages – the final section was built around 1700.

Sunnybank Hall is probably the earliest timber house in the area. It was originally known as Over Nabroyde and was held by Thomas De Hollinedge. The name was derived from the fact that it was above (over) the road to Nab. In 1472, the house was renamed Sunnybank. In 1546, the hall was conveyed to Henry Savile of Bradley Hall. His descendants held the property until 1927.

Snow creates havoc at the bottom of Greetland's Rochdale Road in 1963. The shop was known as Freda's Park Stores and the garage behind is now Brow Bridge Garage.

Mills and public buildings dominate this view of West Vale from Greetland. Victoria Mills, Brig Royd Mill, North Dean Mill and George Ingham's Prospect Mill are all prominent, as is St John's church and the Public Hall. The River Calder and Little London can be seen as we approach Elland.

One of a series of postcards published in the 1930s. It highlights the dominance of Clay House on the village.

Mothers load their children onto excursion coaches for the annual day out from Greetland Dyers WMC around 1956. Centrally are Florence Crouch, Vera Mellor and Elsie Barron.

A wagon loaded with bales of wool lost control in Rochdale Road and embedded itself in the corner of the Park Stores. The gates to Clay House are at the left. The local constabulary assist to evacuate the house, which is in imminent state of collapse.

A timber prop supports the corner of the store and the photograph is labelled to assist recognition.

Red Cross Nurses march down Rochdale Road and are seen passing The Fleece Inn. Middle of the front row is Violet Rawnsley. On her left is May Rawnsley.

Lord Mexborough owned Bradley Mill Farm, together with surrounding land. Tenants had to travel to Mexborough to pay their rents. The property boasted a fine waterwheel. Douglas Williams of Elland lived in the white painted building but it remained unoccupied for many years.

Waste Bridge at Little Bradley. Saddleworth Road runs left to right centrally behind Fielding's Mill.

Woodfield Mill, Saddleworth Road, Greetland. It was built in 1870 by Benjamin Fielding and was acquired in 1951 by J. & E. Bentley. This was the family of Dr Phyllis Bentley, the well-known author. The mill closed in 1979 due to the depressed state of the textile trade.

Clay House barn from the rear on 14 February 1981. Just weeks away from demolition, the barn was saved and restored. The unusually attractive form of the barn and its large size is testimony to the wealth and importance of the Clay family. Part of the barn is said to have been used as a place of worship during the nineteenth century.

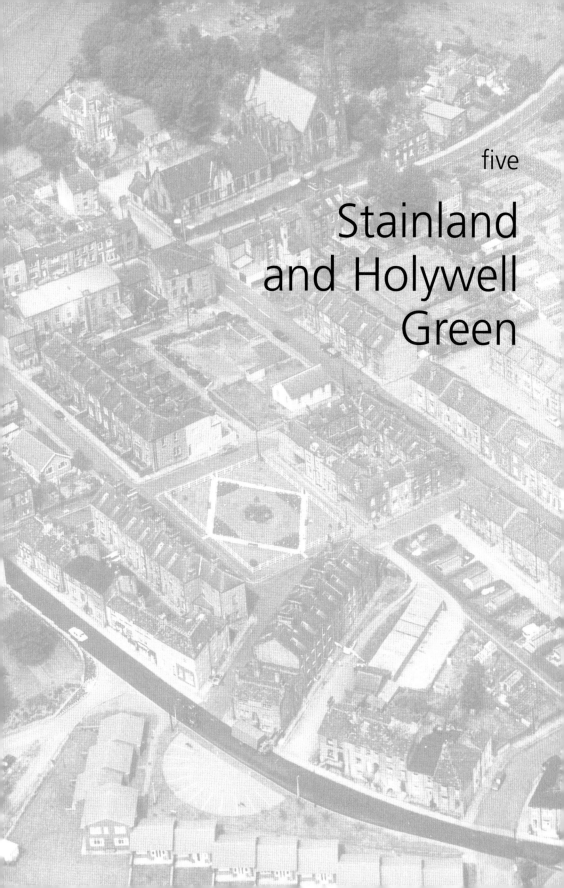

five

Stainland and Holywell Green

Stainland Road, running along the top of this photograph, was built as a turnpike road in 1825. Station Road, running from top left to bottom right, was originally a track to Elland. Travellers had to use the ford at Holywell Brook. At the bottom of the photograph are the bungalows erected in 1969 on the site

of St Helen's Square, a collection of seventeenth-century buildings. The Shaw family moved the holy well to St Helen's Square about 1855 when they diverted the water supply for their new dyeing plant. It originally stood at Mellor Mill Lane.

Holywell Green Tollhouse in 1869. The inn next door was known as the Wagon and Horses before becoming the Station Hotel and latterly the Holywell Inn. The road to the left drops significantly into Holywell Brook and to the right to West Vale.

A similar view sixty years later. The trams arrived in 1921 but horse-drawn traffic is still in evidence as the animal patiently awaits its driver.

October 1978 and Holywell Green Congregational church is being demolished.

Stainland Road passes Burwood Mills and Holywell Green church. The railway viaduct is seen centre left.

Workmen laying tramlines to Holywell Green. Trams began running to Stainland in 1921. Private buses commenced running in 1926. The building on the right is Burwood Mill, once owned by the Booth family who were local farmers.

Stainland Road looking towards West Vale. The building on the left after the houses is the Ingwood Mill of J. Speak.

Looking down Station Road with St Helen's Square at the bottom. In the external wall the outline of a barn door can be clearly seen.

Holywell Brook, busy with traffic. The Rock Inn is positioned centrally. The road to the left leads to Holroyd's Mill and further to Bedlam and Rhodes and Horrocks' Mill before reaching West Vale. Blackley chapel, and chimneys associated with the brickworks, can be seen on the horizon.

A multi-view postcard of Stainland. This 1960s card still shows wide-open spaces, which are gradually disappearing.

A view of Bowling Green. The High Street is in the centre with Well Royde off to the right. The shop on the left was Shaw's chemist. The three-storey building in the centre was formerly the Gardener's Arms.

Samuel Rothwell Godhard, a local Methodist preacher, lived in the house to the left of the cross, which had railings at this time.

At some time the cross was moved and erected at its present location. Originally it was probably a meeting place or a preaching cross used by itinerant priests before churches were built. The Stainland Cross resembles the description given for the Elland Cross.

On 23 May 1895 a terrific explosion occurred at Holme Mill, which was situated at the foot of a slope leading up to Shunts Wood. The *Echo* and *Halifax Guardian* reported the event under the heading 'Stainland Calamity'.

The explosion occurred at 1.30 p.m. Men from a nearby tenter field rushed to help rescue victims. Doctors Nicholson and Woodcock attended but sadly five women were fatally injured, including Mary Connelly, aged nineteen, who had started work at the mill that very morning.

Onlookers viewed the bodies of the victims, now covered by a sheet. Those killed were Mary Connelly, nineteen, Eliza Booth, nineteen, Sarah Wood, forty-six, Merrena Goodwin, twenty-two, and Bessie Bentcliffe, eighteen.

This shop was situated next door to the Bull and Dog in South Parade. It had previously been a barber's shop owned by George Wright Iredale. Next door was Goddard's butchers shop and next door but one the fish and chip shop of Clay Thomas. Pictured left to right in the shop doorway are: Miss Mary Anne Wade, Mrs Martha Wade, Mr J. Wade and Miss Annice Wade.

Stainland with High Street on the left leading to Beestonley Lane and eventually Barkisland. The house on the right is Well Royd, built in 1762, and once the home of the Schofield family. Both father and son were solicitors. The gateposts seen further down the road are at the entrance to Scholes Farm and the large building directly behind the lamp standard was the Congregational church vicarage.

six

North Dean Mill

North Dean mill was built in 1876/77 as a steam powered woollen mill. The main mill is of four storeys and it had an internal end engine house with an attached boiler house and chimney. A house and offices were added in 1878 and a warehouse in 1885. The mill was further extended in 1919.

Office staff and management in 1964 included left to right: Christine Ramsden, Vera Sanderson, Cynthia Smithies and manager Ernest Welbourne. Until the early 1940s the business was Joseph Smith & Sons and it then became Hoyle (Greetland) Ltd. Sam Hoyle was chairman of the company and his fellow directors included his sons Edmund and Charlie. Later his grandson Sam Robinson Hoyle joined the board.

The Sam Robinson Hoyle Memorial Garden. The garden and shelter were given to the former Elland Urban District Council by Edmund and Mrs Hoyle of North Dean Mill.

The site of the garden was formerly occupied by Stainland Road Methodist church. The church was opened in 1841 and closed in 1946. The freehold of the land was sold for £100, the stone for £205 and the slates for £250. A glass vestry screen was sold for £4. The church was demolished in 1952.

Left: The garden was given in memory of Lt-Col. Sam Robinson Hoyle, a former CO of the 7th Battalion, Duke of Wellington's Regiment. After his military service, during which he won the Military Cross, Col Hoyle returned to North Dean Mill as managing director. Sam Robinson Hoyle died in 1952 aged thirty-four.

Below: Here we see four generations of the Hoyle family. The baby is Richard Martin Robinson Hoyle. The others are, left to right: S. R. Hoyle, Edmund Hoyle, and Sam Hoyle. Sam Hoyle founded garage businesses in Halifax, Huddersfield and Hebden Bridge, calling his company Trinity Garages.

Opposite: 'Conditions in this year, 1947, look pretty bad and many businesses are distressed and as hopeless as this little chap. However, things will improve if we all pull together and give of our best. Can we help you in any way?'

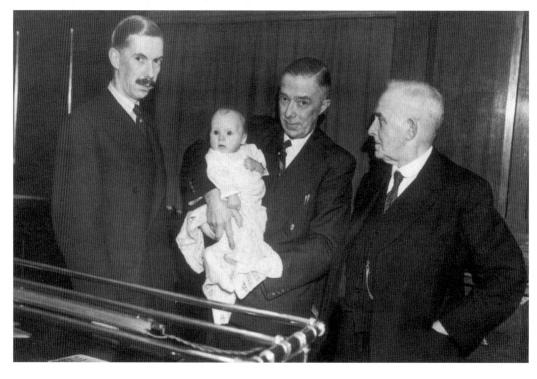

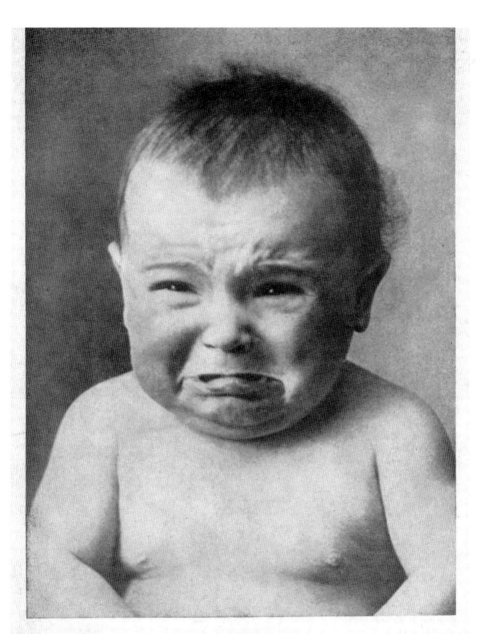

"1947"

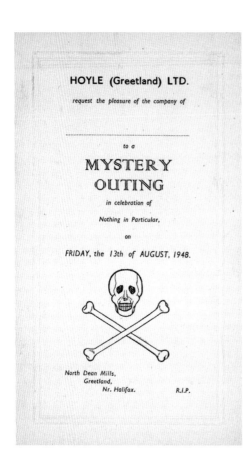

HOYLE (Greetland) LTD.

request the pleasure of the company of

....

to a

MYSTERY
OUTING

in celebration of

Nothing in Particular,

on

FRIDAY, the 13th of AUGUST, 1948.

North Dean Mills,
Greetland,
Nr. Halifax.   R.I.P.

Left: It seems management required very little in the way of an excuse to close the mill down for the day and transport their employees to the seaside, the Lake District or a pantomime. Everyone was fêted, wined and dined at the firm's expense. Wedding anniversaries, coming of age, births and birthdays, all warranted a trip out. Indeed one invitation dated Friday 13 August 1948 was organised to celebrate 'nothing in particular'.

Below: A group of employees have just enjoyed lunch at Windermere Hydro on Friday 2 October 1959. A trip on the lake, a call at Morecambe to view the illuminations and a drinks stop on the way home amounted to a very convivial day out.

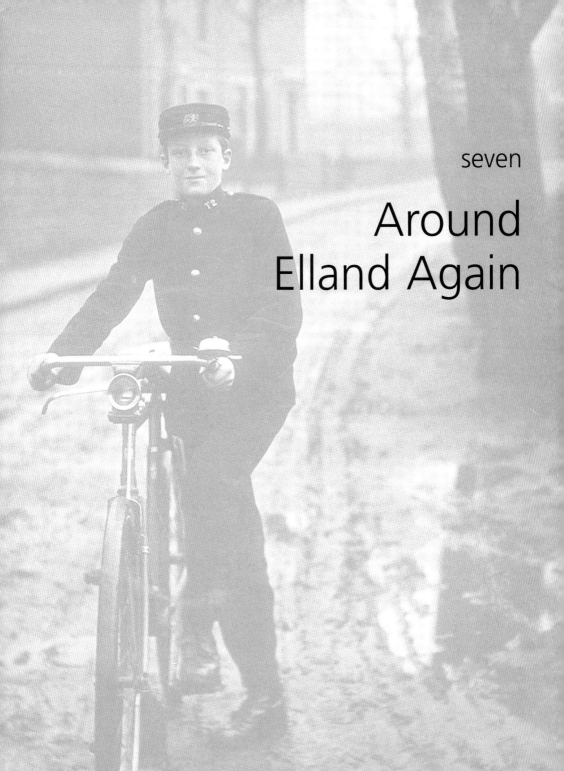

seven

Around
Elland Again

Taken from the north-west this aerial shot allows a view of most of Elland. The foreground includes
West Vale School, Prospect Mill, the Public Hall and St John's church. The river winds into Elland

accompanied by Saddleworth Road, Long Wall and Hullen Egde Road. The Ainleys (Huddersfield Road), Upper Edge and Lower Edge are clearly recognisable, as is Elland Bridge.

Savile Road shines like a ribbon centrally. South Lane is in the foreground and All Saints' church and Norton Mills dominate the middle of this view from Ainley Fields. The ancient footpath from Ainley Top to Elland Bridge can be seen on the right.

A Joe Dean vehicle negotiates Hullen Edge Road in August 1972 for the Elland Carnival. The St John's Ambulance man is Derek Crouch.

The tram carries the date 30 May 1914. This image was issued to draw attention to the deficiencies of the tram network between Huddersfield, Halifax and the surrounding area.

Two young girls and two boys stand for the photographer at The Cross. Clues as to the date include the fact that St Mary's church clock has more than one face and the shops looking into Southgate have yet to have their upper sections redesigned.

Looking into Southgate from The Cross in 1903. The buildings shown remain basically intact after 103 years. The Savile Arms is on the right. The entrance to Box Hall Road is central and to the right.

War memorial at Hullen Edge. The break in the wall at the right is a viewpoint which allows extensive views of the Calder and Ryburn valleys.

The footpath from Ainley Top can be clearly seen and, if followed, it eventually leads to Elland Bridge. Dempster's Engineering Works are on the right and other mills can be seen in South Lane (6 August 1940).

Children take it easy for the photographer in Ainley Woods. The footpath negotiates the steep hillside towards Ainley Top, *c.* 1902.

From the early days of steam, the Waterhouse siding signal box lies in the valley between Elland and Brighouse on the Yorkshire and Lancashire line. It stands at the foot of Lower Edge hillside.

The girls assist with haymaking in Ainley Fields. Rosemount is to the right and Park Wood dominates the skyline.

A young James Brearley delivers letters or telegrams in Whistons Lane. James later became an auctioneer and valuer in Elland.

A post office worker wheels his barrow of parcels from Elland railway station over Elland Bridge, up the steep Northgate and into Southgate. The buildings at The Cross have yet to be renovated.

Ainley Top before the M62 was built. In the early days of motor transport Elland firms added as much as three quarters of an hour to their time to allow for negotiating this hill. Today this stretch of road is about four times wider.

Trams in tandem on Route No. 7 at The Ainleys.

The carriage waits outside The Rawson's Arms in Park Road. This public house closed in the later years of the twentieth century and after refurbishment the building is part of the business premises of W. T. Knowles Pipeworks.

Several establishments and organisations take part in these seasonal notes at Elland.

Although Bethesda church has remained unchanged, this corner of Victoria Road, Jepson Lane and Savile road is much altered. Acre Mead now occupies the open space in the foreground and the Sunday school was demolished in 1999. This opened up the vista of the main entrance to Bethesda.

Danesbury House in Timber Street. This building was demolished in 1881. Timber Street was formerly known as Lucy Street after a lady resident.

Where Stainland Road crosses the river Calder between Calder and Hebble and North Dean there stood this tollhouse. Livestock were driven along the road where a toll was paid at this bar. Pedestrians had to pay at one period and this stretch of road is still known locally as the 'Ha'penny Bar'.

A general view of the Elland Bridge area, Gog Hill to the right, Kiln End Mills to the left and St Mary's church overshadowed by the hillside of Upper Edge and The Ainleys.

Elland in the horse-and-cart era at the bridge; Elland Hall dominates this area. The road still has Yorkshire setts.

A church procession makes its way to St Mary's church in 1955. The high wall protects Ellen Royd from prying eyes and the Hammer and Pincers Hall is situated centrally. (Photograph by Maurice Robson.)

Eddie Conley with a group of musicians who played for dances and concerts in the 1930s. The drummer is Jack Banks, who was a mechanic and engine tenter at Elland Finishing Company in South Lane.

eight

School Days

South End Boys Standard 4, 1953. Top row left to right: Malcolm Green, Graham Waddington, David Holdsworth, -?-, Richard Dyson, Chris Garrett, Christopher Dearden, David Horsfall, Derek Jenkins, Rodney Short, Alan Stansfield. Middle row: Mr Frank Meadow Sutcliffe (class teacher), -?-, Colin North, -?-, Roger Swift, David Longbottom, Gordon Douglas, John Highley, David Slater, -?-, David Weston, David Garside, Mr A. Kemp (headmaster). Front row: Barry Royston, Malcolm Ross, David Tooby, David Thornton, Ronald Sykes, Michael Driver, Derek Fleming, Peter Robinson, David Owen, Phillip Chadwick, Peter Hallas.

The young man in his Eton collar stands with friends in New Street when celebrations for the Coronation of King George V and Queen Mary were taking place in 1912.

The earth toilets that were used at the National School until the early 1950s.

The towels hang in an orderly fashion as the little girl washes up the school crockery at the National School in the 1950s.

Employees of Albert Bailey's of Riverside Mill and their children prepare for a day out in Blackpool in 1951. Alistair and Trevor Williamson are on the right with Nigel Southern next to them. Michael Moss, in a very smart school cap, is fifth from the left in the front row. Others pictured include Fred Crabtree, Harold and Ivy Southern, Hazel, Ethel and Annie Moss.

Miss Milnes class, Church of England School, 1953. Back row: -?-, Jimmy Wright, Kenneth Pilling, David Lumb, Frederick Abbott, Howard Norcliffe, Trevor Crowther, Billy Smith, George Hawkins, Brian Wright, Tony Botterill, Barry Law, Tony Stockings, Alan Belgrave. Middle row: David Cushing, Melvin Sadler, Roger Longbottom, Joan Beverley, -?-, Jacqueline Hunter, Susan Longbottom, Pat Rodgers, Margaret Drury, Pamela Adams, Glenys Banks, Evelyn Carey, Anthony Sharp, Lewis Mitchell. Front row: Gwyneth Powell, Jacqueline Waterworth, Melita Harrison, Hazel Holroyd, Enid Stott, Dorothy Richards, Sandra Marsden, Sylvia Laverty.

This anonymous group are posing round about 1900. The presence of a minister, extreme left, suggests a religious group of some sort.

These children look seriously at the camera. The boys mostly have lace or Eton collars and the girls are mainly in pinafore dresses. The buttoned tunics perhaps indicate a church organisation.

The cameraman, perhaps enquiring what this 1914 gathering was about, opportunely caught these two lady cyclists. The background is dominated by Elland Hall, which was demolished during the construction of Calderdale Way, the Elland bypass.

A more distant view of Elland Bridge includes Sunday school scholars walking down Long Wall towards West Vale and Greetland, the ladies in their fine hats, gents in their straw boaters and the children in their finest clothes. It is perhaps a Whitsuntide gathering.

nine

Nu-Swift

The Nu-Swift factory in Wistons Lane. The original Nu-Swift extinguisher was manufactured in 1926 by Blakborough & Son of Brighouse In 1933 the Nu-Swift Engineering Co. was formed and moved to premises in Elland Lane.

These people are employed as assembly testers and are currently processing eighty-three charges. In 1936 the Wistons Lane factory was acquired. It was originally a woollen mill built around 1863 and known as Whitwell Mill.

The tool room is a hive of activity and a member of the management, Robert Grotte, in the white overall, is pictured centrally. At the extreme left is Gordon Wilson who retired in 2005 after more than fifty years service to Nu-Swift.

Extinguisher cases stand like the terracotta army waiting to be painted. The original mill was burned down in 1877. It was rebuilt and taken over by a firm of cotton doublers, Wadsworth & Fairbank, in 1907. It closed in 1930.

All extinguishers were subjected to a final air test as illustrated here. With the woollen and cotton industries offering exceptional fire risks it is little wonder that Nu-Swift prospered.

People obligingly look towards the cameraman for this shot of the welding shop, known as the 'backoyle'. It is noticeable that working women still wore skirts as opposed to today's more socially acceptable trousers and jeans.

A demonstration of the height attainable by this operative beside 'Braintree'. The business developed rapidly in the early years of the war and F. Graucob Ltd acquired it in 1943. Number of employees: 150.

Periodically people were brought in for advertising work. Here a woman handles her extinguisher towards a fire. In the background is the Low Laithe Slaughterhouse and the Gas Holder. Albert Bailey's mill is to the right.

Two lines of fire are set up for this publicity still. The chimney of Riverside Mill stands sentinel over the background and a signal stanchion can be seen for trains approaching Elland Station.

A British Road Services vehicle leaves the Nu-Swift site with a consignment for the Royal Canadian Navy. During the Second World War, the Nu-Swift Universal was chosen and standardised on all the King's ships.

John Costello is involved in loading a vehicle with material for overseas. Not all production was for export. Extinguishers were sold to the National Coal Board, the textile industry, bus companies, farmers and fish fryers as well as to offices and homes.

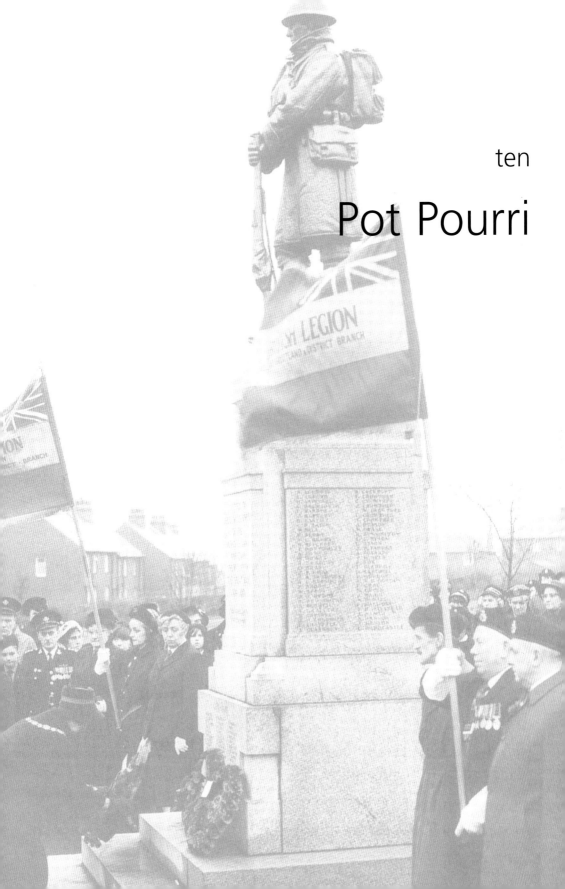

ten

Pot Pourri

Post Office Corner, Barkisland. In 1937 the wooden hut on the right was a butcher's shop occupied by Willie Barker. His father was the Greetland 'Bobbie'. Before this it was a barber's shop.

The same junction under heavy snow in 1947.

Right: Joseph Smithies & Son Ltd built these houses for his employees in 1875, next door to Albert Mills, Saddleworth Road.

Below: There were twelve back-to-back houses at the same level as Saddleworth Road, and six houses at the River Calder side at a lower level.

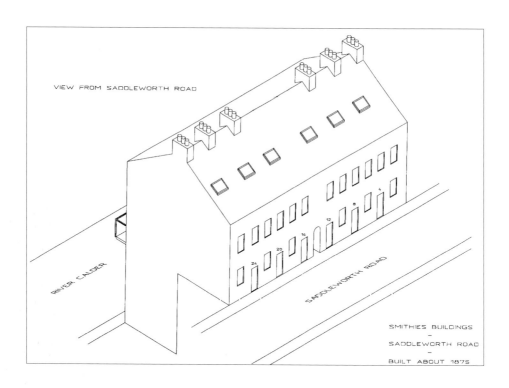

VIEW FROM SADDLEWORTH ROAD

RIVER CALDER

SADDLEWORTH ROAD

SMITHIES BUILDINGS
–
SADDLEWORTH ROAD
–
BUILT ABOUT 1875

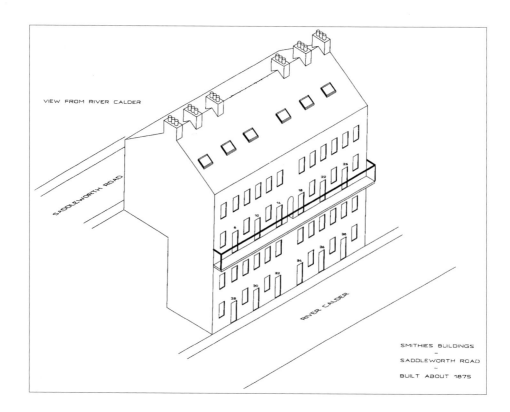

VIEW FROM RIVER CALDER

SADDLEWORTH ROAD

RIVER CALDER

SMITHIES BUILDINGS
–
SADDLEWORTH ROAD
–
BUILT ABOUT 1875

Boating on the River Calder in May 1916. The Brookfoot conurbation is clearly seen and the houses at Grove Terrace look brand spanking new.

Opposite above: The coal man had a choice of eighteen coal grates in Saddleworth Road. Access to houses at the rear was down twenty-six steps, but for dustbin emptying and removing, access was allowed through the mill.

Opposite below: Residents included Eleanor Proberts at No. 16. Fred Kaye lived at No. 26 and worked at Albert Mill for forty years. Gladys Walmsley lived at No. 30 and Mary Midgely lived at No. 36. Her father James W. Raby was a famous champion walker who at one time held thirteen world records.

Above: A view of The Cross and the lower entrance to Westgate. Manchester House is now occupied by the Forrest family, and the shop that was Beaumont's is now enclosed. The bank building is at the junction of Northgate and The Cross.

Left: Service of Remembrance at Hullen Edge Park, 13 November, 1966. Mrs Cawdry, chairperson of Elland Urban District Council, lays a poppy wreath. Members of Elland, Greetland and District branch of the British Legion, St John's Ambulance Brigade and other organisations are in attendance.

The Red Lion Inn, Stainland. The derelict property around the inn has been cleared. During the Second World War, Herbert Brook was licensee. He lost a leg in an accident involving a tram in West Vale during the early 1930s.

A beautifully posed photograph by the workers at John Shaw's Holywell Brook depot at the turn of the twentieth century. The crates conjure up images of the world at large: Melbourne, Sydney, Newcastle, Haiphong...

A view of industrial Elland in the Bridge area. Gashouse or Gas Works Lane runs left to right in the foreground. The Valley Mills of John Dewhirst dominate in the middle distance and the Park Road mills of Benjamin Whiteley. The houses of Plains Lane are seen below the grassland leading to the crematorium.

Opposite above: Two mounted policemen sample local ice cream during the sweltering carnival of 1976. After leading the carnival procession through Elland they take a well-earned rest in Hullen Edge Road.

Opposite below: Fred Haigh was licensee of The Star Inn New Street, prior to its closure in 1966. Here he is with customers left to right: Eric Greenwood, Michael Cleary, Mohammed Razan, Fred Haigh, with Johnny Bates in front, Harold (Ted) Wilson, George Dyson.

Workmen prepare the ground off Elizabeth Street for the building of Elland Baths. The fire and ambulance stations were housed in the building with the water tower around 1900.

The frontage of the Wainwright Hall has been much changed since this photograph was taken in 1959. The front wall has been removed and a porch entrance has been built. The two nurses are perhaps encouraging people to attend a blood collecting session.

Mrs Kathleen Cawdry, chairperson of Elland Urban District Council, lays a wreath in Elland Council Office Garden on the 9 November 1966. The minister is the Revd Frederick Drummond Sykes, vicar of St John's church, West Vale.

The 1920s and the Merry Pom-Poms of West Vale pose for a publicity shot by Murduck, photographer of South End, Elland.

Lower Edge Road winds into Elland passing Lodge Drive and Lodge Avenue. The Elland Lane Estate is in the middle distance and new estates now occupy much of the land in-between.

Trams pass each other at the bottom of Salterhebble Hill. The nearest tram is proceeding to the terminus at the Shears Inn, West Vale. The Punch Bowl Inn is on the extreme right.

Church Street, Elland in around 1908. House painters are busy at the lower end of the street. The building in the foreground had previously been The Red Lion Inn from which coaches ran to many towns.

The junction of Huddersfield Road and South Lane in around 1907. This area had previously been known as Withens Gap, and before Huddersfield Road was built, South Lane was the main route to Huddersfield.

The horse and trap dominate this scene but it also includes a girl with a child in its perambulator, two children on the right and a gentleman in a bowler hat, c. 1908.

9 January 1992 and long-serving employees of the Central Electricity Generating Board at Elland Power Station gather for a reunion at The Fleece Inn. Left to right: Paul Thornton, Roy Mitchell, Ken Chadwick, Joe Coop, Albert Bradley, Alan North, Ray Swift. Seated front: Bill Holroyd, Reg Parker.

Turner was a chimney sweep and a soot collector. The telephone number is perhaps an indicator of how telephone technology has advanced.

eleven

And in Conclusion…

With Fondest Love
from
ELLAND

If there's one thing I wish......
......more than anything else,
And one thing I'd like to do:
It's just to shake hands and tell you I wish,
Many happy returns to You......

Posted from No. 17 South Lane, Elland and wishing all the best to 'Friends', it is signed by 'The Dysons' and dated September 1904.

Alas, poor Elland! In the days
When Elland air was clean and sweet
And quaint old houses met the eye
Along its winding street

The 'postcard craze' was all unknown
With many another modern fad
And neither pencil sketch nor sun
Copied the grace it had

Now the old town that once was ours
The home of childhood's happy days
Is to us but an early dream
Seen in a golden haze

So, ere last fragments of old stones
Old hills, old woods we loved so much
Crumble to dust 'neath greed of gold
Or folly's idle touch

I bring you pictures, one or two
Which may recall, for blame or praise
Faint memories of a fairer place
The Elland of the olden days.